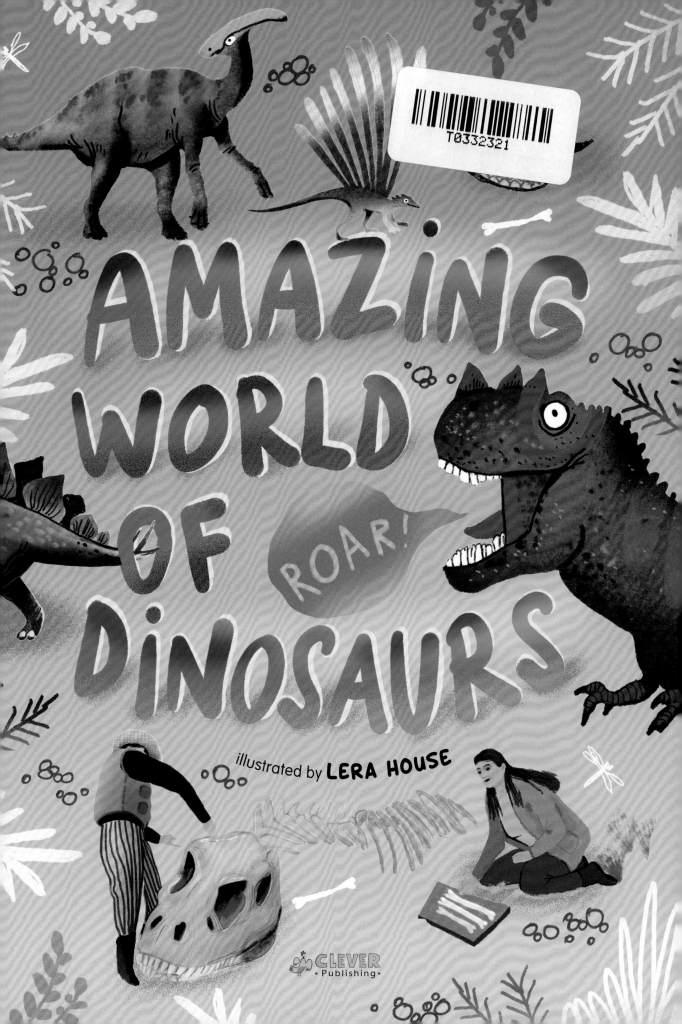

AMAZING WORLD OF DINOSAURS

ROAR!

illustrated by LERA HOUSE

CLEVER
Publishing

EXCAVATIONS, BONES, AND SKELETONS

Life on our planet began a very long time ago. Scientists still aren't sure exactly when, but it is believed that the first living cells appeared more than 4.5 billion years ago!

A PALEONTOLOGIST is a scientist who explores the world of the past by studying fossils.

Trapped by heavy layers of sand and mud over millions of years, this skeleton of a dinosaur is well-preserved!

SET OF TOOLS:

brushes

bucket

trowel

WHEN DID DINOSAURS LIVE?

The word "dinosaur" means "terrible lizard."
Dinosaurs first appeared on Earth a very long time
ago and lived for millions of years.

Peteinosaurus

The Earth was covered in
forests. Pine trees, huge ferns,
and giant conifer trees grew all
over the planet.

Coloradisaurus

Dicynodont

Stegosaurus

Longisquama

Prestosuchus

Henodus

Different kinds of dinosaurs existed during three different time period

TRIASSIC PERIOD
(252-201 million years ago)

JURASSIC PERIOD
(201-145 million years ago)

VALLEY OF THE DINOSAURS

Many dinosaur species lived on the planet. There were carnivores, herbivores, and omnivores. Some of them lived on land, and others in the water. A few kinds of flying reptiles dominated the sky.

MEAT EATERS
Tyrannosaurus rex, also known as T. rex, is the most famous of the carnivores, or meat eaters.

PLANT EATERS
Lots of dinosaurs were gentle giants who fed on plants and tree leaves. They were known as herbivores.

CARNIVORES

THE CARNIVORES, or **MEAT EATERS**, fed on other dinosaurs. These prehistoric hunters had huge teeth as sharp as knives. Their muscular legs helped them to run fast.

Ceratosaurus

Carnotaurus

Baryonyx

Tyrannosaurus rex

The jaw of a **T. REX** included 60 serrated teeth, each almost a foot long. They are the longest dinosaur teeth ever found.

HERBIVORES

THE HERBIVORES,
or **PLANT EATERS,** fed on plants and leaves from trees. Dinosaurs with a long neck, armor, or a collar walked on four large and round feet that support their heavy weight. Some could even stand on two feet!

Diplodocus

Mamenchisaurus

Pachycephalosaurus

Iguanodon

This giant insect was a **MEGANEURA,** a prehistoric dragonfly.

MARINE REPTILES

ELASMOSAURUS didn't swim fast, but its long neck helped it catch fish.

Tanystropheus

Elasmosaurus

Eurhinosaurus

Mosasaur

ARCHELON was the biggest marine turtle that ever existed.

The **MOSASAUR'S** jaw was full of razor-sharp, hooked teeth.

Archelon

FLYING REPTILES

Feathered or not, giant creatures with wings were kings of the sky. They were very good at climbing and flying, and some were the size of a small airplane.

DIMORPHODON ate insects and lizards.

Dimorphodon

Scaphognathus

DINO DEFENSE

Dinosaurs had different ways to protect themselves. Armored dinosaurs had horns, spikes, or plates, and many had long, spiked tails.

Amargasaurus

Chasmosaurus

Triceratops

Ankylosaurus

This dinosaur's spines were covered by skin.

DINOSAUR YOUNG

Many dinosaurs laid eggs in nests. The adults took care of their babies, brought them food, and protected them from predators.

THE END OF THE DINOSAURS

More than 66 million years ago, dinosaurs disappeared from the Earth. Scientists think a gigantic meteorite hit the planet and created a huge dust cloud that blocked the sunlight. Without light and heat, the dinosaurs couldn't survive.